The MAILBOX®

Word Family HELPERS

Fun · Word-Building Practice for Beginning Readers

- **Word lists**
- **Craft ideas**
- **Individual activities**
- **Group activities**

- **Cards**
- **Patterns**
- **Skill sheets**

Spelling · Vocabulary · Phonics · Fluency

Managing Editor: Lynn Drolet

Editorial Team: Becky S. Andrews, Diane Badden, Catherine Broome-Kehm, Kimberley Bruck, Karen A. Brudnak, Pam Crane, Sarah Foreman, Pierce Foster, Tazmen Hansen, Marsha Heim, Lori Z. Henry, Lucia Kemp Henry, Debra Liverman, Kitty Lowrance, Jennifer Nunn, Gerri Primak, Mark Rainey, Kelly Robertson, Hope Rodgers, Eliseo De Jesus Santos II, Donna K. Teal, Rachael Traylor, Sharon M. Tresino

www.themailbox.com

©2010 The Mailbox® Books
All rights reserved.
ISBN10 #1-56234-929-5 • ISBN13 #978-1-56234-929-5

Printed in the United States
10 9 8 7 6 5 4 3 2 1

HPS211918

TABLE OF CONTENTS

What's Inside......................................3

Single Word Families

Multiple Word Families

WHAT'S INSIDE

⭐ Practice with single word families

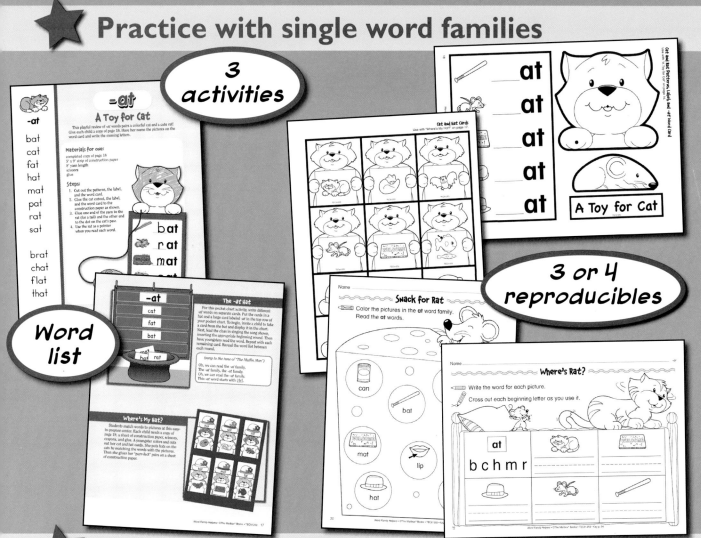

3 activities

Word list

3 or 4 reproducibles

⭐ Practice with multiple word families

-an

ban

can

fan

man

pan

ran

tan

van

bran

plan

span

than

A Friendly Fan

Youngsters spin this fan to practice reading -an words. To begin, give each child a copy of page 6. For each picture on the fan, have him write the onset and trace an.

Materials for one:

completed copy of page 6   brad
7" construction paper circle   scissors
6½" construction paper square   glue

Steps:

1. Cut out the fan pattern and the label.
2. Glue the label near the bottom of the square. Glue the fan to the circle.
3. Set the circle atop the square and use a brad to connect the pieces.

A Friendly Fan

An -an Can

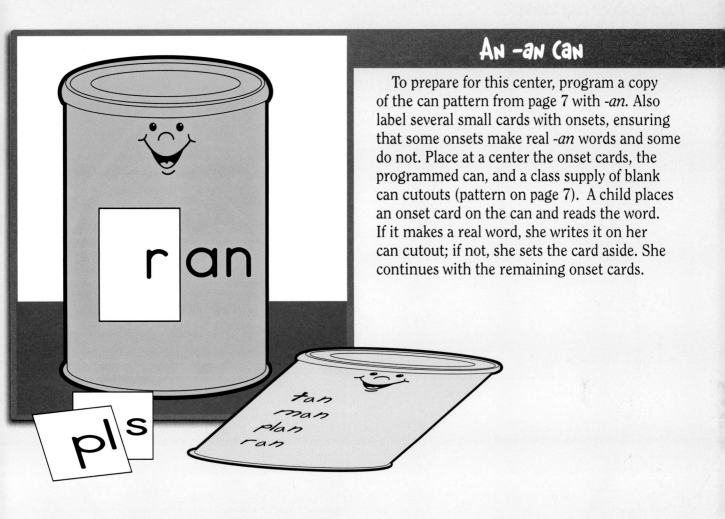

To prepare for this center, program a copy of the can pattern from page 7 with -an. Also label several small cards with onsets, ensuring that some onsets make real -an words and some do not. Place at a center the onset cards, the programmed can, and a class supply of blank can cutouts (pattern on page 7). A child places an onset card on the can and reads the word. If it makes a real word, she writes it on her can cutout; if not, she sets the card aside. She continues with the remaining onset cards.

Stop the Van!

For this group activity, have each child cut out a copy of the van pattern on page 7 and glue it to a large craft stick. To begin, draw a road on the board within students' reach. Write words along the road, ensuring that some of the words are -an words and some are not. Then invite a student to "drive" his van along the road. When he gets to a word, he stops and reads it aloud. If the word is in the -an word family, all the students hold up their vans. If it is not, they do nothing. After checking for accuracy, invite a different child to the board to "drive" to the next word. Continue until the end of the road is reached.

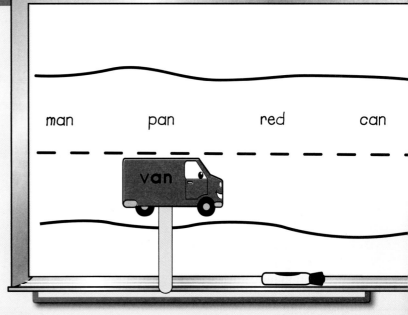

___an

an

an

an

an

TEC61253

A Friendly Fan

☐ ☐ ☐ ☐ ☐

Class   Creature

Students read -ap words to beat a fictitious opponent in this group game! Put a cutout copy of the game cards on page 13 in a cap. On chart paper, draw a child and a creature, each wearing a ten-sectioned cap, and label them as shown. To begin, lead students in the rhyme shown. Then pass the cap to a child, have him remove a card, and have him read the word aloud. If the word ends with -ap, he colors a section on the class cap; if it does not end with -ap, he colors a section on the creature's cap. Then he returns the card to the cap. Continue until one cap is completely colored.

nap   cap   mat   ap   clap

> Read a word that's in our cap.
> Did you find a word with -ap?

Tap the -ap Word!

Write on chart paper several -ap words and a few without -ap. To begin, lead youngsters in singing the song shown. Then invite a volunteer to tap an -ap word with a decorative pointer. If he is correct, have him circle the word with a crayon; if not, guide him to conclude that the word selected does not end with -ap and have him cross out the word. Continue until each -ap word has been identified.

(sung to the tune of "London Bridge")

Let's tap a word that ends with -ap,
Ends with -ap, ends with -ap.
Let's tap a word that ends with -ap.
Who can find one?

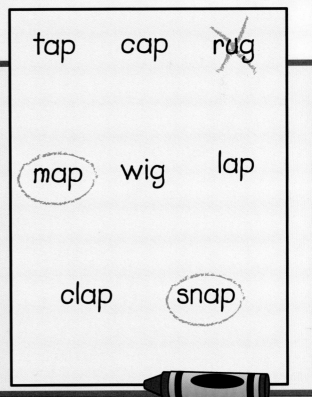

tap   cap   rug

map   wig   lap

clap   snap

Cap Pattern and Onset Strip

Use with "Flap Cap" on page 10.

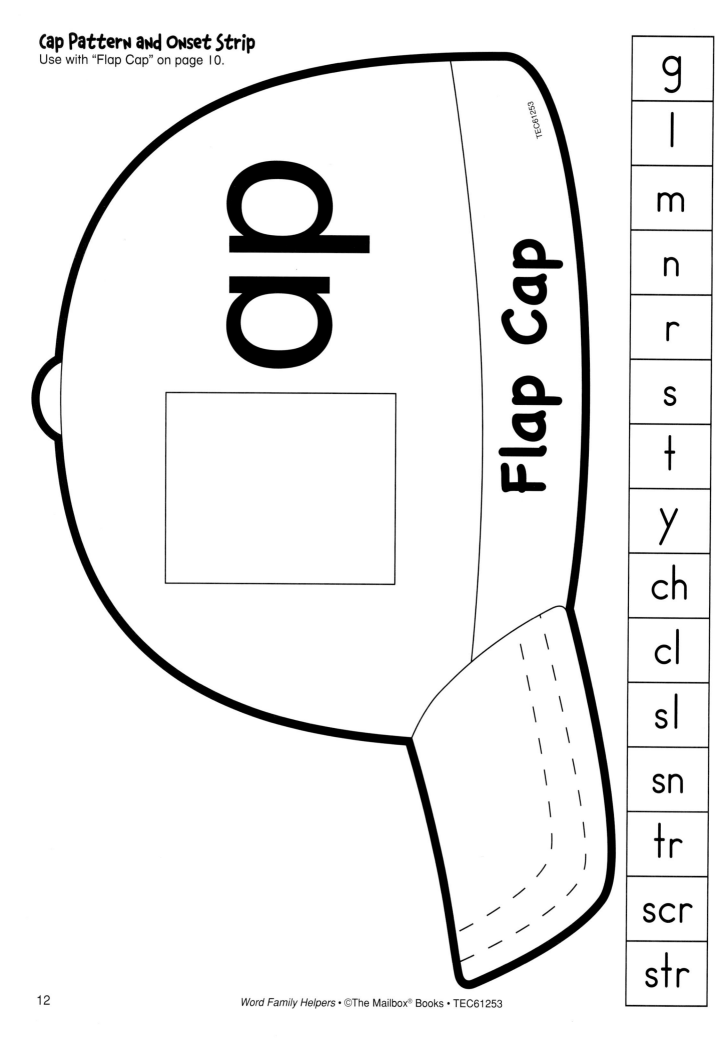

TEC61253

ap

Flap Cap

g
l
m
n
r
s
t
y
ch
cl
sl
sn
tr
scr
str

12   *Word Family Helpers* • ©The Mailbox® Books • TEC61253

cap

lap

map

nap

tap

clap

flap

slap

snap

trap

bug

mat

pan

sad

TEC61253

Time to Nap

Trace the **ap** words.

Cut.

Glue to match.

map

lap

cap

nap

snap

clap

Word Family Helpers • ©The Mailbox® Books • TEC61253 • Key p. 94

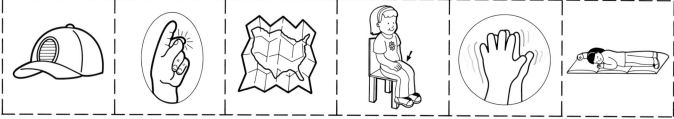

The -at Hat

For this pocket chart activity, write different -at words on separate cards. Put the cards in a hat and a large card labeled -at in the top row of your pocket chart. To begin, invite a child to take a card from the hat and display it in the chart. Next, lead the class in singing the song shown, inserting the appropriate beginning sound. Then have youngsters read the word. Repeat with each remaining card. Reread the word list between each round.

(sung to the tune of "The Muffin Man")

Oh, we can read the -at family,
The -at family, the -at family.
Oh, we can read the -at family.
This -at word starts with [/b/].

Where's My Hat?

Students match words to pictures at this easy-to-prepare center. Each child needs a copy of page 19, a sheet of construction paper, scissors, crayons, and glue. A youngster colors and cuts out her cat and hat cards. She puts hats on the cats by matching the words with the pictures. Then she glues her "purr-fect" pairs on a sheet of construction paper.

Cat and Rat Patterns, Label, and -at Word Card

Use with "A Toy for Cat" on page 16.

A Toy for Cat

TEC61253

at at at at at

Word Family Helpers • ©The Mailbox® Books • TEC61253

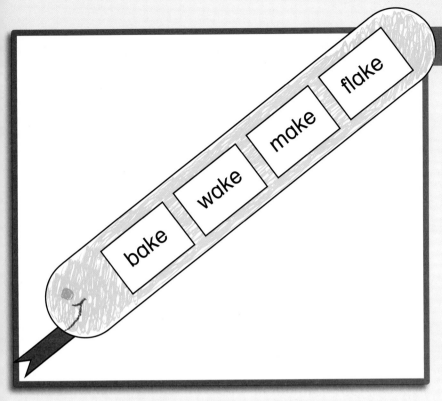

The student-made snakes at this center are covered with -*ake* words. Place at a center student copies of the word cards from page 25, a class supply of 2" x 12" paper strips, red paper scraps, scissors, crayons, and glue. A student rounds the corners of a paper strip, draws a face, and glues on a red paper tongue so the strip looks like a snake. Then she cuts out the word cards and reads each word. If it is an -*ake* word, she places it on the snake. If it is not, she sets the card aside. Then she glues the -*ake* words in place. **For an added challenge,** have each student write more -*ake* words on the back of her snake.

A Yummy Cupcake

Prior to beginning this group-time activity, give each child a copy of the cupcake pattern (precut the slits) and the onset strip from page 25. Have him decorate the cupcake and then cut out the cupcake and strip. Next, keeping the letters forward, help him thread the strip through the slits and glue the ends together. To begin, name an -*ake* word from the cupcake. Ask each student to slide the strip to form the named word. After scanning for accuracy, announce another word. **To extend the activity,** have each child write the words on a sheet of paper to make an -*ake* word family.

Picture Cards, Label, and Cake Pattern

Use with "Take Some Cake" on page 22.

TEC61253

Take Some Cake

TEC61253

TEC61253

cake

rake

lake

snake

shake

flake

TEC61253

TEC61253

TEC61253

Word Family Helpers • ©The Mailbox® Books • TEC61253

Word Cards
Use with "Make a Snake" on page 23.

wake	make	bag
TEC61253	TEC61253	TEC61253
bake	name	flake
TEC61253	TEC61253	TEC61253

| | ake
TEC61253

l
sn
t
r
r
br
fl
m
w
c

Glue here.

-ake

Shake to Go

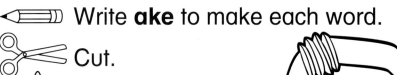

✏️ Write **ake** to make each word.

✂️ Cut.

Glue to match.

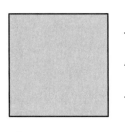

r _____

c _____

l _____

sn _____

fl _____

-ay
Play in the Hay

The hay bales in this wagon provide a quick review of -ay words. To begin, give each child a copy of page 29. Then have each youngster write a different -ay word on each hay bale card. (Provide help as needed.)

Materials for one:

completed copy of page 29
9" x 12" construction paper
3" x 9" construction paper
scissors
glue

Steps:

1. Cut out the label, handle pattern, and hay bale and mouse cards.
2. Round the bottom corners of the 3" x 9" construction paper (set horizontally) and glue it near the bottom of the 9" x 12" construction paper as shown.
3. Draw wheels near the bottom of the 3" x 9" paper. Then glue the handle and label in place.
4. Glue the hay bale and mouse cards to look like they are in the wagon.

-ay
day
hay
lay
may
pay
ray
say

clay
play
stay
tray

spray

-ay
day
tray

A Friendly Jay

What does the blue jay say? Find out at this center! Cut out a tagboard copy of the blue jay pattern and onset wheel from page 30. Use a brad to attach the wheel behind the blue jay where indicated. Place the blue jay and writing materials at a center. A child writes *-ay* at the top of a sheet of paper. Then she spins the wheel to make a word, reads it, and writes it on her paper. She continues in this manner to form an *-ay* word family.

What Do You Say?

To begin this whole-group activity, write a word (either in the *-ay* word family or not) on the board. Encourage students to silently read the word. Then ask, "What do you say? Is it an *-ay?*" If a child thinks the word is from the *-ay* word family, he gives a thumbs-up; if not, he gives a thumbs-down. After scanning for accuracy, invite a youngster to read the word aloud. Then erase the word and write a different one to play again.

Play in the Hay

TEC61253

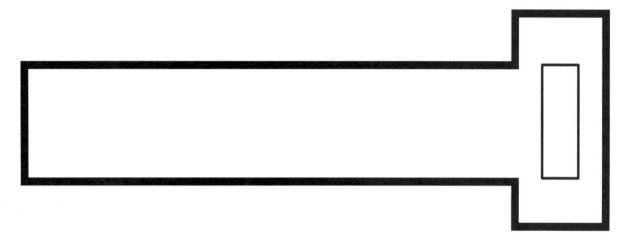

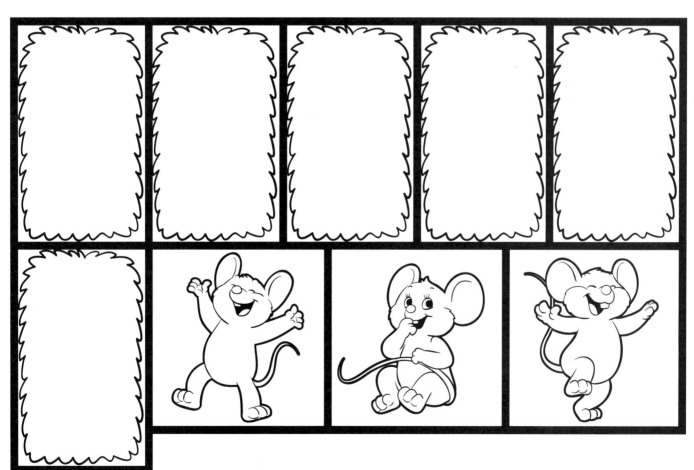

Word Family Helpers • ©The Mailbox® Books • TEC61253

Dessert Tray

 Trace.

Write **ay** to make each word.

d _____

st _____

h _____

s _____

l _____

p _____

m _____

pl _____

-ed

bed

fed

led

red

wed

bled

fled

shed

sled

sped

shred

-ed
A Cozy Bed

This project helps students distinguish between real and nonsense *-ed* words. To begin, have each child read the words on a copy of page 34 and then lightly color each real word.

Materials for one:

completed copy of page 34
two jumbo craft sticks
construction paper
scissors
glue

Steps:

1. Cut out the bed pattern and cards.
2. Glue the colored cards to the bed. (Discard the uncolored cards.)
3. Glue the bed to the construction paper and then trim around it to make a border.
4. Glue a craft stick to each end of the bed to make bedposts.

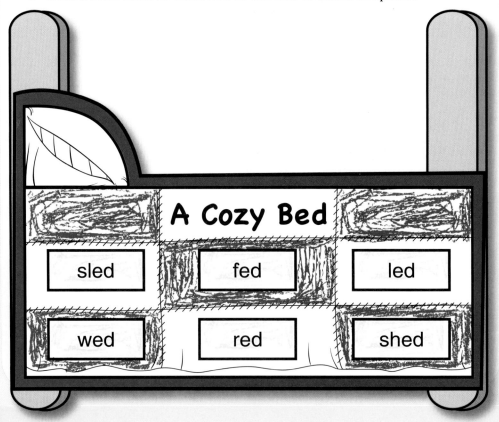

Bed Booklet

These simple-to-make booklets give youngsters practice reading and writing *-ed* words. Have each child color and cut out a copy of the booklet backing and pages from page 35. Direct her to stack the booklet pages behind the letter *b*, place them atop the backing, and staple them on the left. Then guide her to flip through each page and blend the onset with *-ed* to read the word. After she reads each word, have her write the words on a sheet of paper to make an *-ed* word family.

On the Sled

Place at a center a class supply of 6" x 9" construction paper sheets, a hole puncher, yarn, scissors, and crayons. Also place at the center a set of word cards, some labeled with *-ed* words and some with words from different word families. A child uses the provided materials to make and label a sled similar to the one shown. Then he chooses a card and reads the word. If it is an *-ed* word, he writes it on his sled. If it is not, he sets the card aside. He continues with the remaining word cards.

Bed Pattern and Word Cards

Use with "A Cozy Bed" on page 32.

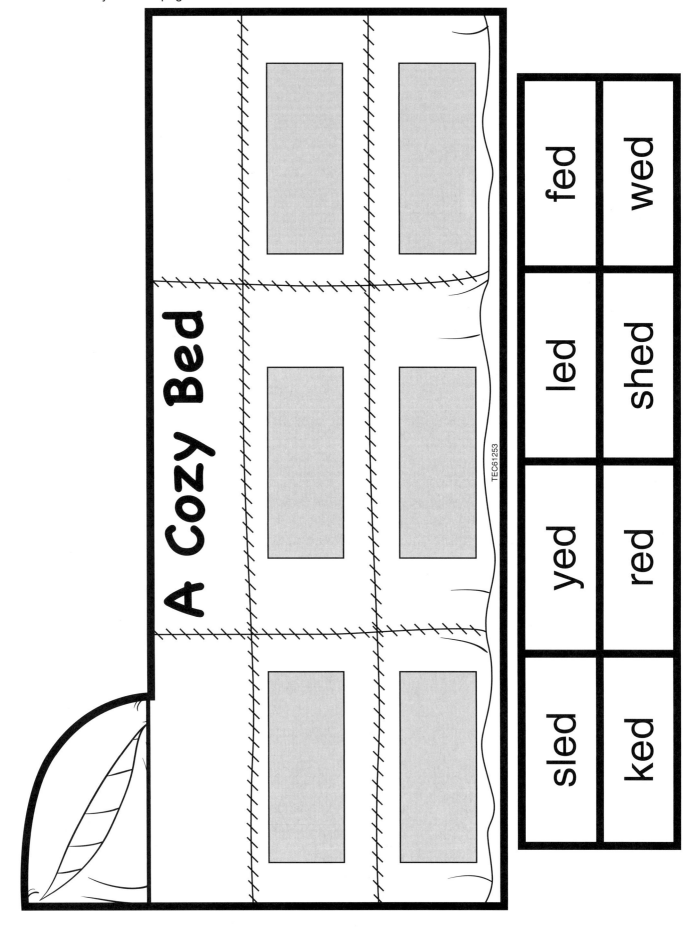

A Cozy Bed

TEC61253

| fed | led | yed | sled |
| wed | shed | red | ked |

Word Family Helpers • ©The Mailbox® Books • TEC61253

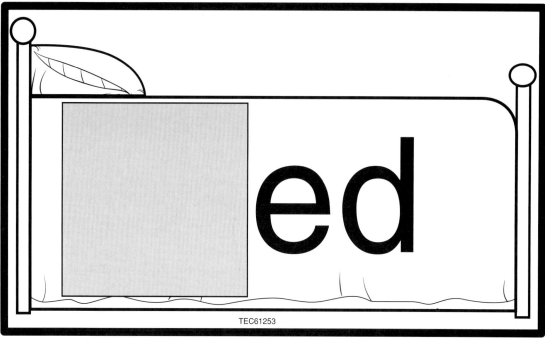

TEC61253

b	f	l
r	w	bl
fl	sh	sl

Roses Are Red

Color the **ed** words red.

wed

led

pan

bed

pig

pot

sled

bled

fled

cat

fed

shed

-et
Get the Net!

It's fun to catch *-et* words in this net! To begin, have each child trace the words on the butterfly cards on a copy of page 39.

Materials for one:
completed copy of page 39
6½" x 7" construction paper
1" x 7" construction paper strip
scissors
glue

Steps:
1. Fold the 6½" x 7" construction paper (set vertically) in half and glue the sides to make a pocket.
2. Cut out the cards and label, and glue the label to the front of the pocket.
3. Round one end of the construction paper strip to make a handle and glue it in place.
4. Round the bottom corners of the pocket so it looks like a net.
5. After you read the word on each card, place it in the net.

-et

bet

get

jet

let

met

net

pet

set

vet

wet

yet

fret

Fish in a Net

To prepare for this small-group activity, copy and cut out a fish card from page 40 for each group member. Label each fish with either a word from the -et word family or a word from a different word family. Also obtain a net. To begin, invite a student to read the word on a fish and determine whether it is an -et word. If it is, he places the fish in the net. If it is not, he sets the card aside. Continue until each child has had a turn.

High-Flying Jet

As students spin the wheel on this jet, they blend onsets with -et to form words. Copy the jet and letter wheel from page 40 for each student. (Precut the small square on the jet.) Have each child cut out the patterns and then place the letter wheel behind the jet so the dots align. Help her insert a brad through the dots. Then have her turn the wheel, read each -et word, and write the words on a cloud cutout.

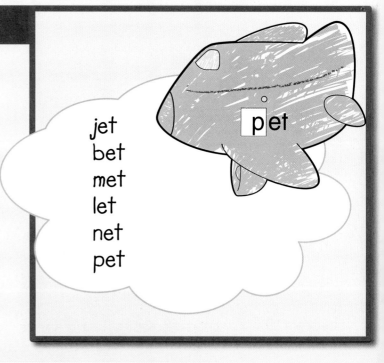

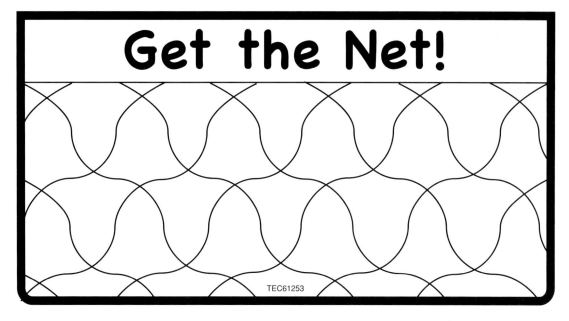

Get the Net!

TEC61253

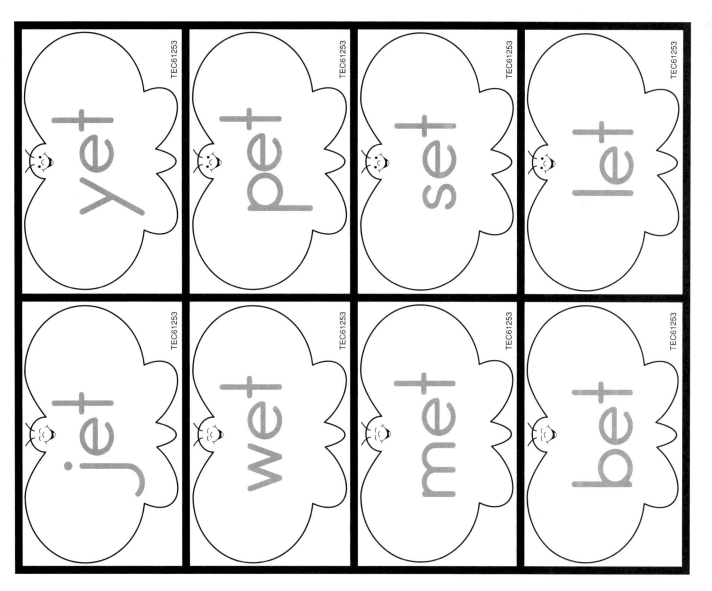

Jet Pattern and Letter Wheel
Use with "High-Flying Jet" on page 38.

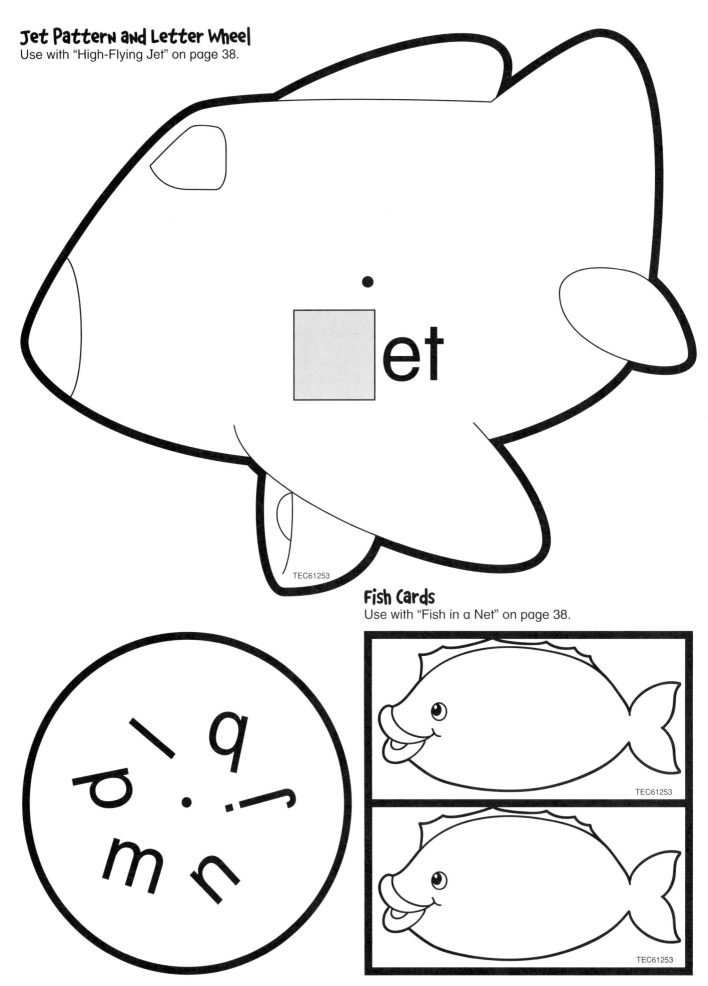

˙et

TEC61253

Fish Cards
Use with "Fish in a Net" on page 38.

l
q
p
j
m
n

TEC61253

TEC61253

Word Family Helpers • ©The Mailbox® Books • TEC61253

A Big Dig

Youngsters dig for *-ig* words at this center. To prepare, cut apart a tagboard copy of the cards from page 45. Place brown paper shreds (soil) in your sensory table or a large plastic tub and bury the cards in the soil. Also set at the center a plastic pail and shovel. A child digs up a card and reads the word. If the word is from the *-ig* word family, she places the card in the pail. If it is not, she sets the card aside. To extend the activity, the child removes the cards from the pail and writes the words on a sheet of paper to form an *-ig* word family.

Raise the Twig

To prepare for this whole-group activity, draw a large twig on chart paper and write the title shown. Also gather a class supply of small twigs from outside. To begin, announce a word. If it is from the *-ig* word family, students raise their twigs. Invite youngsters to spell the word as you write it on the chart. If the word does not end in *-ig,* students place their twigs on the ground. Continue until there are several words on the chart.

-ig Word Family

big
dig
twig
wig

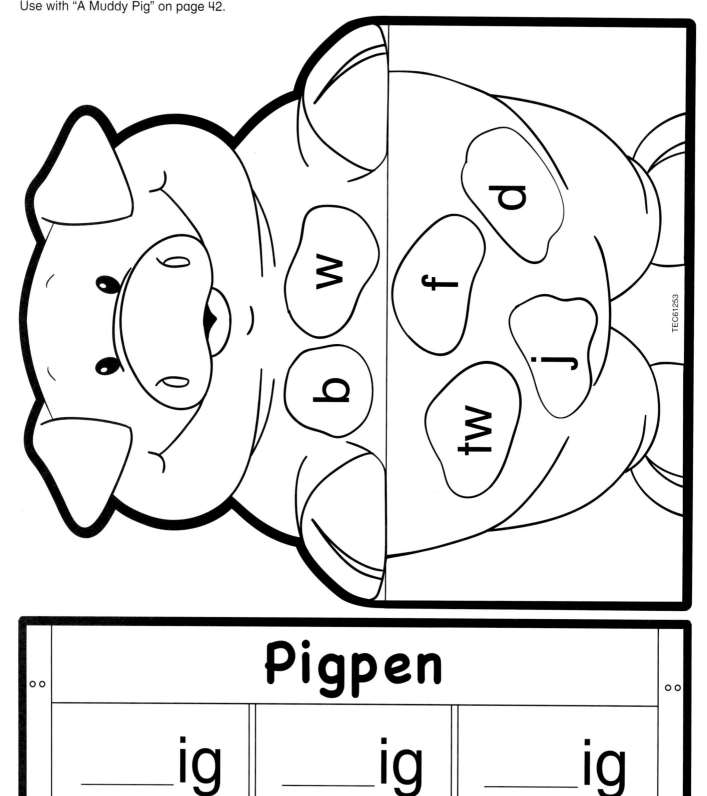

TEC61253

Pigpen

___ig	___ig	___ig
___ig	___ig	___ig

TEC61253

Word Family Helpers • ©The Mailbox® Books • TEC61253

 big

dig

 pig

 twig

 wig

 bed

  map

 pot

TEC61253

TEC61253

TEC61253

TEC61253

TEC61253

TEC61253

TEC61253

TEC61253

A Big Rig

Circle the real **ig** words.

Write.

big wig hig rig pig twig dig

-ig

Word Family Helpers • ©The Mailbox® Books • TEC61253 • Key p. 95

-in

Fin Frenzy

The shark in this ocean scene is the leader of an *-in* word family. Give each child a copy of page 49. Have him write *-in* on each fin to complete each word.

Materials for one:

completed copy of page 49
9" x 12" sheet of light blue construction paper
two 3" x 12" strips of dark blue construction paper
scissors
glue

Steps:

1. Scallop-cut one long edge of each paper strip so it resembles waves.
2. Cut out the patterns and the label.
3. Glue the bottom edge of the shark and each fin behind the wave strips (taking care to keep the words visible). Glue the waves and the label to the light blue paper as shown.

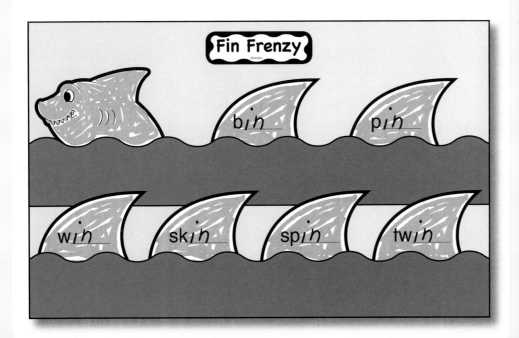

-in

bin

fin

pin

tin

win

chin

grin

shin

skin

spin

thin

twin

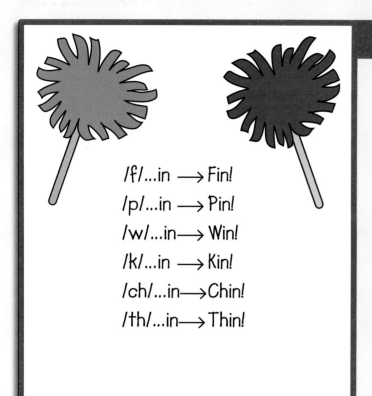

/f/...in ⟶ Fin!

/p/...in ⟶ Pin!

/w/...in ⟶ Win!

/k/...in ⟶ Kin!

/ch/...in ⟶ Chin!

/th/...in ⟶ Thin!

Blend In!

This phonological activity encourages all students to form -*in* words. Practice with youngsters the cheerleader-style chant shown. Then repeat the chant for several rounds, inserting different onsets that make real words with the -*in* rime. **To differentiate real and nonsense words,** include onsets that do not form real words and have youngsters identify each blended word accordingly.

Leader	Group Response
When I say [/f/],	We say in!
[/f/]	in.
[/f/]	in.
What's the word?	[Fin]!

In or Out?

Copy the cards on page 50 so there is one card for each student. Arrange the cards facedown in a circle and invite each child to sit behind a card. To begin, a youngster picks up the card in front of him and reads the word aloud. If the word ends with -*in,* the class says, "Spin in!" and he spins to the middle of the circle, lays the card on the floor, and returns to his seat. If the word is not an -*in* word, the class says, "Stay out!" and he walks around the outside of the circle, returns to his seat, and puts the card facedown behind him. Play continues until each player has had a turn.

Spin in!

win

TEC61253

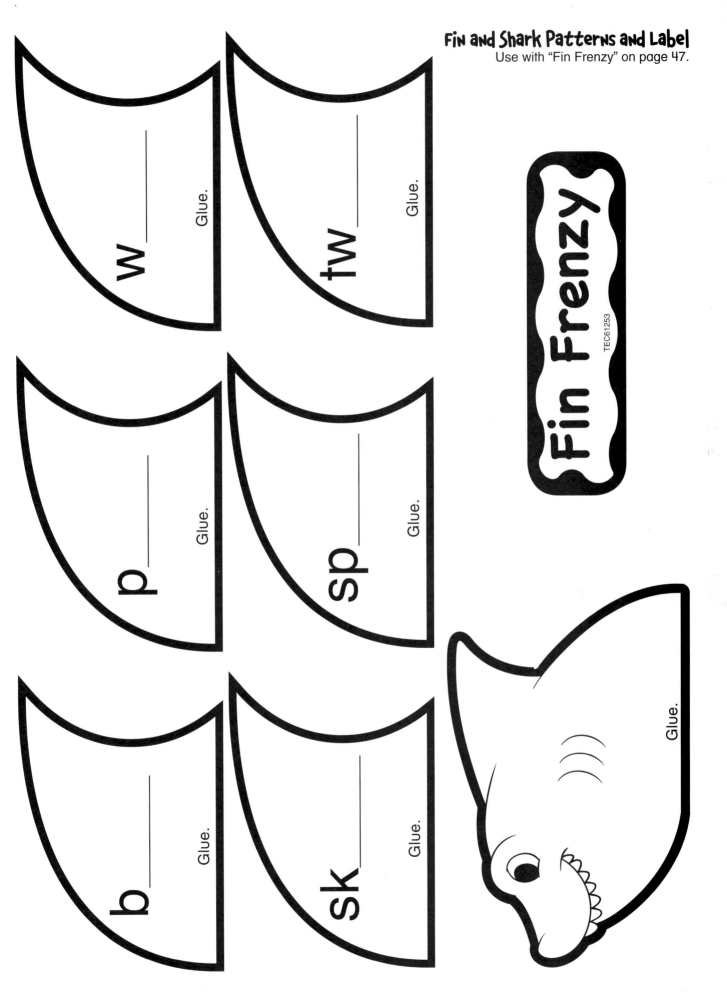

w ___
Glue.

tw ___
Glue.

p ___
Glue.

sp ___
Glue.

b ___
Glue.

sk ___
Glue.

Fin Frenzy
TEC61253

Glue.

fin

TEC61253

pin

TEC61253

win

TEC61253

chin

TEC61253

grin

TEC61253

twin

TEC61253

can

TEC61253

pig

TEC61253

sun

TEC61253

A Warm Grin

Write **in** to make each word.

Cut.

Glue to match.

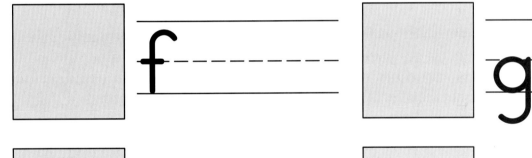

	f ___		gr ___

	p ___		tw ___

	w ___		sp ___

-ip

dip

hip

lip

rip

sip

tip

zip

chip

drip

flip

ship

trip

Ship on a Trip

The cargo on this ship includes a load of *-ip* words. To begin, give each child a copy of page 54. Encourage him to use the word bank, as needed, to label each porthole picture with its matching *-ip* word.

Materials for one:

completed copy of page 54
4½" x 12" strip of paper
3" x 10" strip of paper
two 2" x 4" strips of paper
crayons
scissors
glue

Steps:

1. Glue the paper strips together, as shown, so they resemble a ship.
2. Cut out the porthole pattern and the label and glue them to the ship. (Discard the word bank.)
3. Trim the sides of the ship at an angle.
4. Draw details as desired.

Ship on a Trip

rip   lip   chip   zip   drip

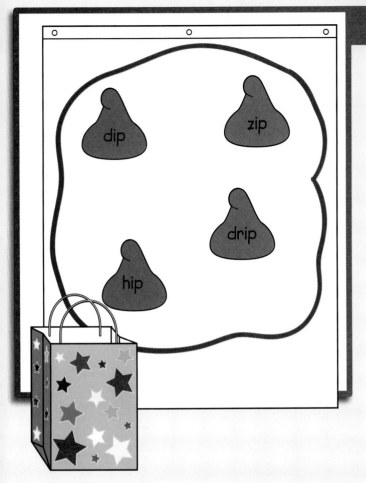

Chocolate Chip Chart

Write a different -*ip* word on each of several chocolate chip cutouts (pattern on page 55); then place the chips in a bag. Draw a large cookie outline on chart paper and then post the chart within students' reach. To begin, invite a student to take a chocolate chip. Next, lead him in the chant shown, inserting the corresponding sounds to read the word on his chip. After he glues the chip to the cookie chart, direct the class to read the word. Continue until each chip has been posted.

> I have a chip!
> *Ip, ip, ip!*
> My word says
> [/h/], *ip*.
> [Hip]!

Kip Takes a Sip

Give each child a copy of the onset strip and rime card from page 55. (Precut the slits on the rime card.) Help her thread the onset strip through the slits. Then name an -*ip* word, using an onset from the strip, and have each youngster pull her strip until the corresponding word is spelled on the cup. Continue with more words as time permits. **For an easier version,** show a matching word card when you name each word.

Ship Label, Porthole Pattern, and *-ip* Word Bank

Use with "Ship on a Trip" on page 52.

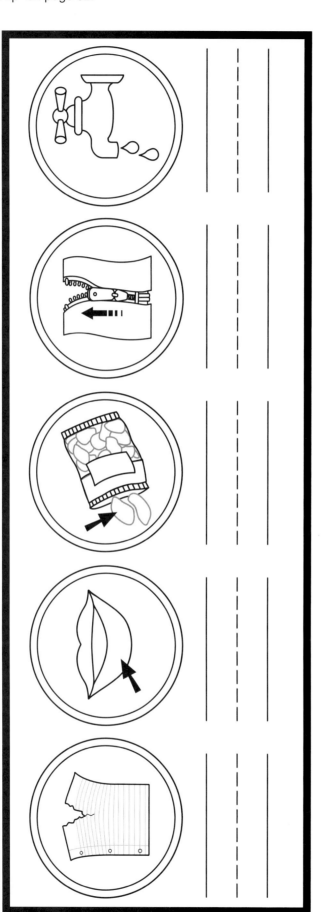

TEC61253

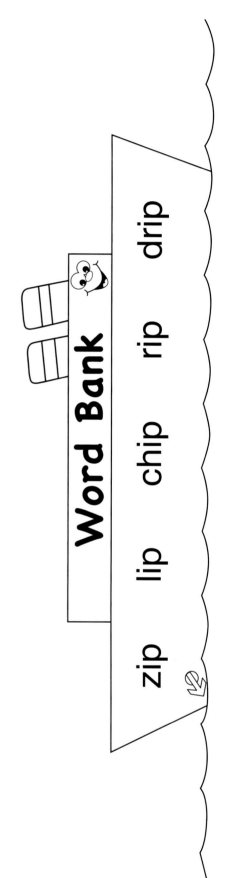

Word Bank

zip   lip   chip   rip   drip

Chocolate Chip Patterns
Use with "Chocolate Chip Chart" on page 53.

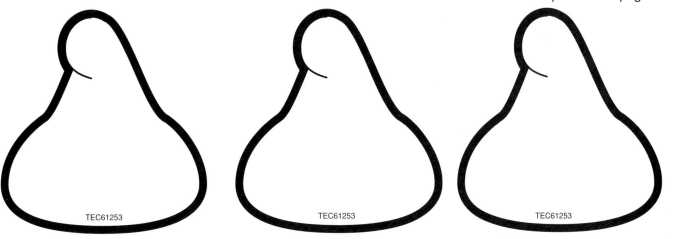

TEC61253   TEC61253   TEC61253

Onset Strip and -ip Rime Card
Use with "Kip Takes a Sip" on page 53.

d	h	l	r	s	t	z	ch	sl	tr

TEC61253

-ip

Hip Hip Hooray!

Cut.

Glue to match **ip** words.

| hip | | rip |

| lip | | ship |

| drip | | zip |

Word Family Helpers • ©The Mailbox® Books • TEC61253 • Key p. 95

-og
A Jog for Dog

As this playful pup "jogs," students practice reading -og words. To begin, give each child a copy of page 59. Have her read the words on the sidewalk stones and then color around each -og word.

Materials for one:

completed copy of page 59
5" x 17" tagboard strip (with a 15" slit across the middle, as shown)
jumbo craft stick
scissors
glue

Steps:

1. Cut out the sidewalk stones, the dog, and the label.
2. Glue the colored stones below the slit on the tagboard strip. (Discard the uncolored stones.)
3. Glue the label above the slit on the strip.
4. Glue the dog to the craft stick.
5. Place the craft stick through the slit. Move the craft stick along the strip so the dog "jogs" along the sidewalk, and read the word on each sidewalk stone.

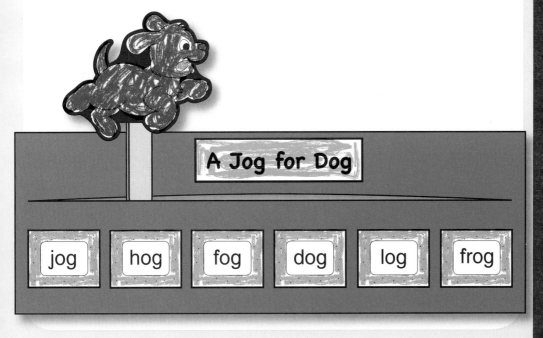

A Jog for Dog

| jog | hog | fog | dog | log | frog |

-og

bog

dog

fog

hog

jog

log

clog

frog

grog

smog

Feed the Dog

The dog at this center eats only -*og* words! To prepare, label a supply of bone cutouts, some with -*og* words and some with words from other word families. Place the bones at a center along with a stuffed dog and a dog food bowl. A child reads the word on each bone. Then she places the -*og* words in the bowl and sets the other words aside. After all the words are sorted, she pretends to feed the bones from the bowl to the dog as she rereads each -*og* word.

Log Cabin

Prior to beginning this group activity, have each youngster write the missing onsets on a copy of page 60. Then direct him to write his name on the cabin, cut out the pages and backing, and staple the pages in place to make a booklet. To begin, announce an -*og* word from the booklet. Ask students to flip to the matching page and read the word. After scanning for accuracy, continue with a different word.

A Jog for Dog

TEC61253

jog	can	log
fog	dog	pen
	rat	frog
	hog	pit

TEC61253

Booklet Backing and Pages

Use with "Log Cabin" on page 58.

_____'s Log Cabin

Word Family Helpers • ©The Mailbox® Books • TEC61253

og

og

og

og

og

og

-og

Frog Fun

✏ Circle each real **og** word.

✎ Write each real word to match.

log   dog

mog   jog   zog

hog   rog   fog   frog

-op

cop

hop

mop

pop

top

chop

drop

flop

plop

prop

shop

stop

Mop It Up!

This friendly mop invites students to match -op words and pictures. To begin, have each child cut out the word cards from a copy of page 64. Then have him read the word on each card and glue it beside the corresponding picture on the mop head.

Materials for one:

completed copy of page 64
1½" x 9" construction paper strip
scissors
glue

Steps:

1. Cut out the mop head pattern.
2. Glue the paper strip to the mop head to make a handle. Then trim the handle to round the top corners.
3. Read each word on the mop head.

Mop It Up!

stop   hop

drop   chop

top   pop

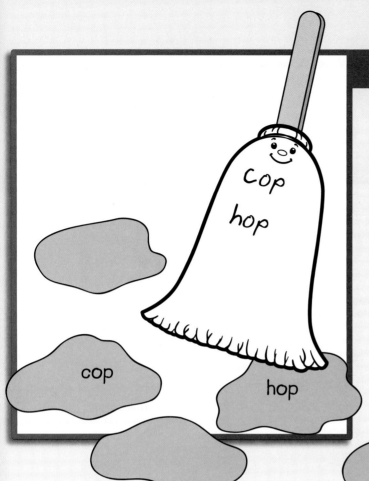

On the Mop

At this center, students mop up -*op* words. To prepare, write real and nonsense -*op* words on blue paper puddle cutouts. Place at a center the puddles, a class supply of mop head cutouts (patterns on page 65), large craft sticks, and glue. A student glues a craft stick to a mop head. Then he spreads out the puddles with the words faceup. Next, he "mops up" a puddle and reads the word. If it is a real word, he writes it on his mop; if not, he turns the puddle over. He continues with each remaining puddle.

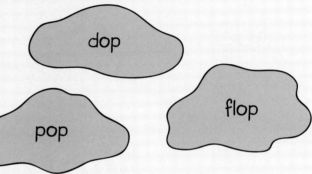

Hop, Hop!

Get youngsters moving while helping them blend onsets with the -*op* rime. To prepare, write -*op* on a sheet of construction paper and secure it to the floor. Write on separate sheets of construction paper different onsets that make -*op* words. Gather students around the rime paper and place an onset next to it. Ask a student to stand behind the onset and hop to the rime as she blends the sounds together to make an -*op* word. Invite other students to hop and read the word. Then continue with different onsets.

/st/-/op/. Stop!

Word Cards and Mop Head Pattern
Use with "Mop It Up!" on page 62.

chop	drop	hop
pop	stop	top

Mop It Up!

-ot

A Pot of -ot Words

This colorful cooking pot holds a quick review of *-ot* words! To begin, have each child trace the *-ot* words on a copy of page 69.

Materials for one:

completed copy of page 69
9" x 12" sheet of construction paper
construction paper scraps

scissors
glue

In advance, cut the construction paper (set vertically) two inches from the top to make two rectangles. Cut a four-inch-wide slit near the top of the larger rectangle.

Steps:

1. Cut out the word list and pot label.
2. Glue the label on the larger rectangle (pot) below the slit.
3. Glue the list to the other rectangle (lid). When the glue dries, carefully thread the list through the slit and pull down to put the lid on the pot.
4. Round the top corners of the lid and the bottom corners of the pot.
5. Cut from construction paper scraps two pot handles and a knob for the lid. Glue the cutouts in place.

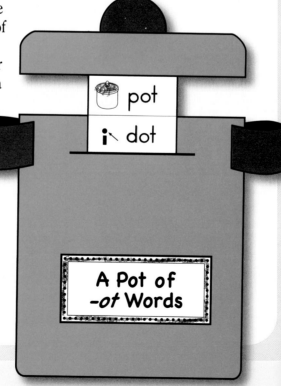

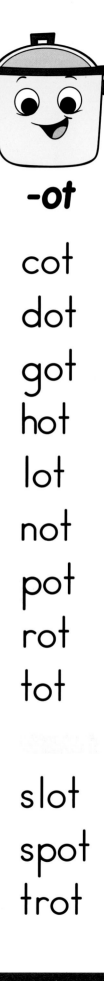

-ot

cot
dot
got
hot
lot
not
pot
rot
tot

slot
spot
trot

A Potful of Practice

To prepare for these group activities, write *-ot* words on individual cards. Place the cards in an empty pot and store the pot near your group area.

- Remove a card without showing the word to students. Say the word's beginning sound. Ask the students to repeat the sound and then say the sound made by *-ot*. Have students blend the sounds to form the word. Finally, display the word for students to read.
- Remove a card. Ask the group to read the word and then ask one child to use the word in a sentence. Set the card aside and repeat the activity with a different card.
- Remove the cards from the pot and arrange them facedown. Have one student select a card and show the word to the group. After the group reads the word, have the student return the card to the pot.

In Full Bloom

Making a flowerpot with *-ot* words is easy! Give each child one card from a copy of page 70 and a 9" x 12" sheet of drawing paper. A student adds the rime *-ot* to each onset to make the words pictured. Next, he cuts out the card and glues it near the bottom of his drawing paper. Then he draws a flowerpot around the card and adds several colorful blossoms.

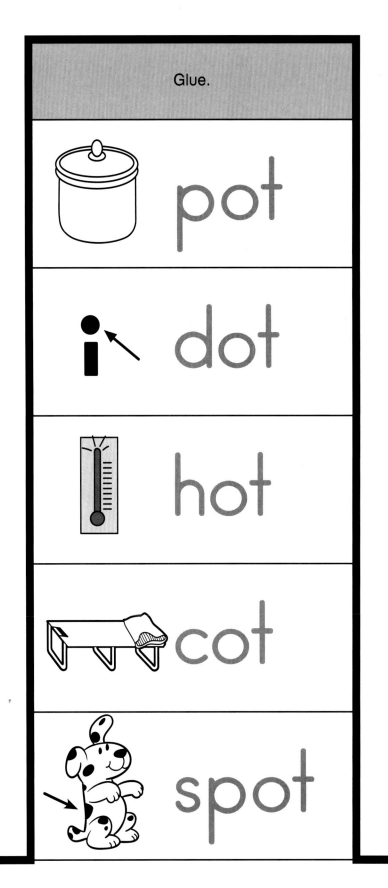

Glue.

pot

dot

hot

cot

spot

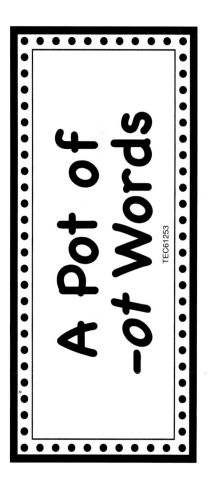

A Pot of
-*ot* Words

TEC61253

Flowerpot Cards
Use with "In Full Bloom" on page 68.

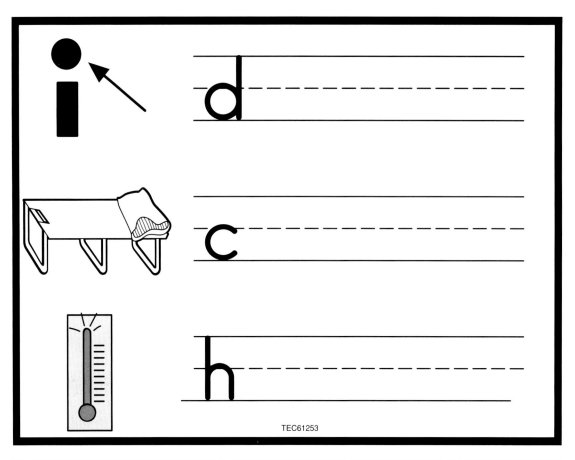

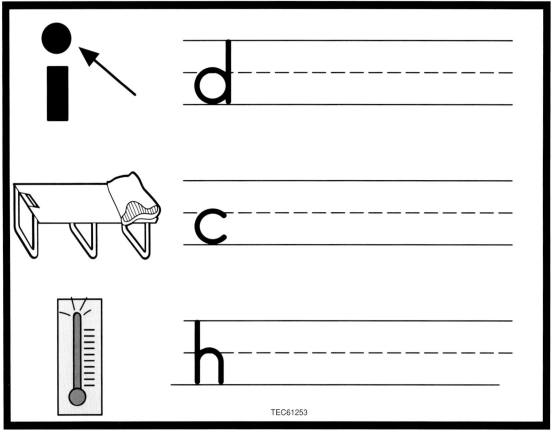

Spot's Lot

Cut.

Glue to match.

pot

cot

hot

tot

dot

Spot

Word Family Helpers • ©The Mailbox® Books • TEC61253 • Key p. 95

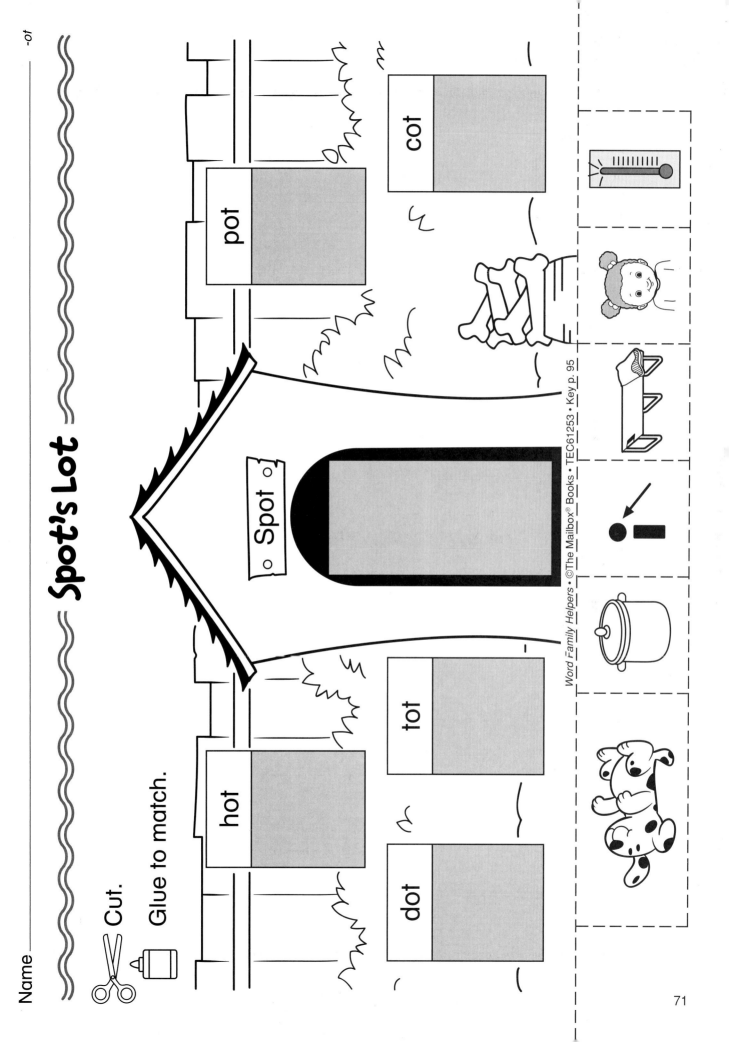

-uck

buck

duck

luck

muck

puck

suck

tuck

cluck

pluck

stuck

truck

struck

-uck
A Pond for Duck

Students are sure to enjoy "walking" this duck with dangling feet on a path of *-uck* words! To begin, have each child trace the onsets on a copy of the word cards on page 74. Then help her read each word.

Materials for one:

completed copy of page 74
2¼" x 24" strip of construction paper
6" x 9" blue paper
2 orange yarn lengths
scissors
glue
tape

Steps:

1. Cut out the word cards, pond label, and duck part patterns.
2. Fold each foot cutout; glue one end of each yarn length in the fold of each foot to make legs.
3. Tape the legs, "walking" right, to the back of the duck.
4. Trim the corners of the blue paper so it resembles a pond. Glue the label to the pond. Then glue the paper strip to the pond so it resembles a path.
5. Glue the word cards to the path.
6. Read each word as you "walk" the duck to the pond.

Stuck.

Waddle Like a Duck!

To begin this action song activity, say a word that ends with the -*uck* rime. Then encourage youngsters to waddle like a duck as they sing the song shown. **For an added challenge,** say two words: one that ends with -*uck* and one that does not. Have youngsters identify the -*uck* word and then sing the song.

(sung to the tune of "If You're Happy and You Know It")

We can hear the -*uck* in [stuck].
  Waddle now!
We can hear the -*uck* in [stuck].
  Waddle now!
We can hear the -*uck* in [stuck].
Waddle, waddle like a duck!
We can hear the -*uck* in [stuck],
  uck, uck, uck!

Stuck Truck

For this group game, cut out the game cards on a copy of page 75. Attach the truck to the side of a shoebox or similar container and place the cards in the box. Divide youngsters into two teams. To start, a player from Team 1 removes a card. If it is a boulder, he reads the word to earn a point for his team; if it says "Stuck Truck," he takes another card, reads the -*uck* word, and earns two points for his team. (Encourage youngsters to seek help from teammates as needed.) Then he returns the card(s) to the box and Team 2 takes a turn. Alternate play continues until each team earns ten points.

Luck.

luck

Word Cards, Pond Label, and Duck Part Patterns

Use with "A Pond for Duck" on page 72.

luck

puck

cluck

truck

duck

muck

tuck

stuck

A Pond for Duck

TEC61253

TEC61253

Word Family Helpers • ©The Mailbox® Books • TEC61253

TEC61253

buck

TEC61253

duck

TEC61253

luck

TEC61253

puck

TEC61253

tuck

TEC61253

yuck

TEC61253

cluck

TEC61253

Stuck Truck

TEC61253

Stuck Truck

TEC61253

Name _____

A Little Stuck

✂ Cut.

🖌 Glue to make **uck** words.

d	l	t uck
st	tr	p uck
	uck	uck
	uck	uck

-ug
Puzzle Bug

This colorful bug showcases the onsets and rime of *-ug* words. Give each child a copy of page 79. Have her trace the onset with one color of marker and the rime with a different color of marker. Encourage her to blend the word parts to read each *-ug* word.

Materials for one:
completed copy of page 79
9" x 12" sheet of construction paper
crayons
scissors
glue

Steps:
1. Cut out the bug patterns and the label.
2. Glue the label at the top left of the construction paper (set horizontally).
3. Assemble the bug parts to make an *-ug* bug and glue them in place. Then draw desired details.
4. "Fly" the bug to a friend and read the words together.

-ug

bug
dug
hug
jug
lug
mug
rug
tug

chug
plug
slug

shrug

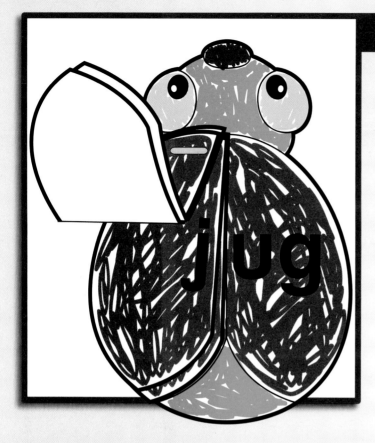

Prior to beginning this group activity, have each youngster color and cut out a copy of the bug booklet patterns on page 80. Help her stack the pages and staple them where indicated to make a booklet. On your signal, invite students to quietly "buzz" around the room with their bug booklets. Then announce a word from the booklet and have students stop and flip to the onset that makes the matching word. After checking the booklets for accuracy, repeat the activity with a different word.

An -ug Mug

To make a mug, give each youngster a large paper square, three paper strips, and a copy of the picture and word cards on page 80. A student rounds the corners of the square so it resembles a mug and then glues on the paper strips to make a handle. Next, he cuts out the picture and word cards and matches each pair. Finally, he glues the pairs to his mug to make an *-ug* word family.

tug

hug

jug

Puzzle Bug

TEC61253

dug

mug

rug

Bug Booklet Patterns
Use with "A Bug Booklet" on page 78.

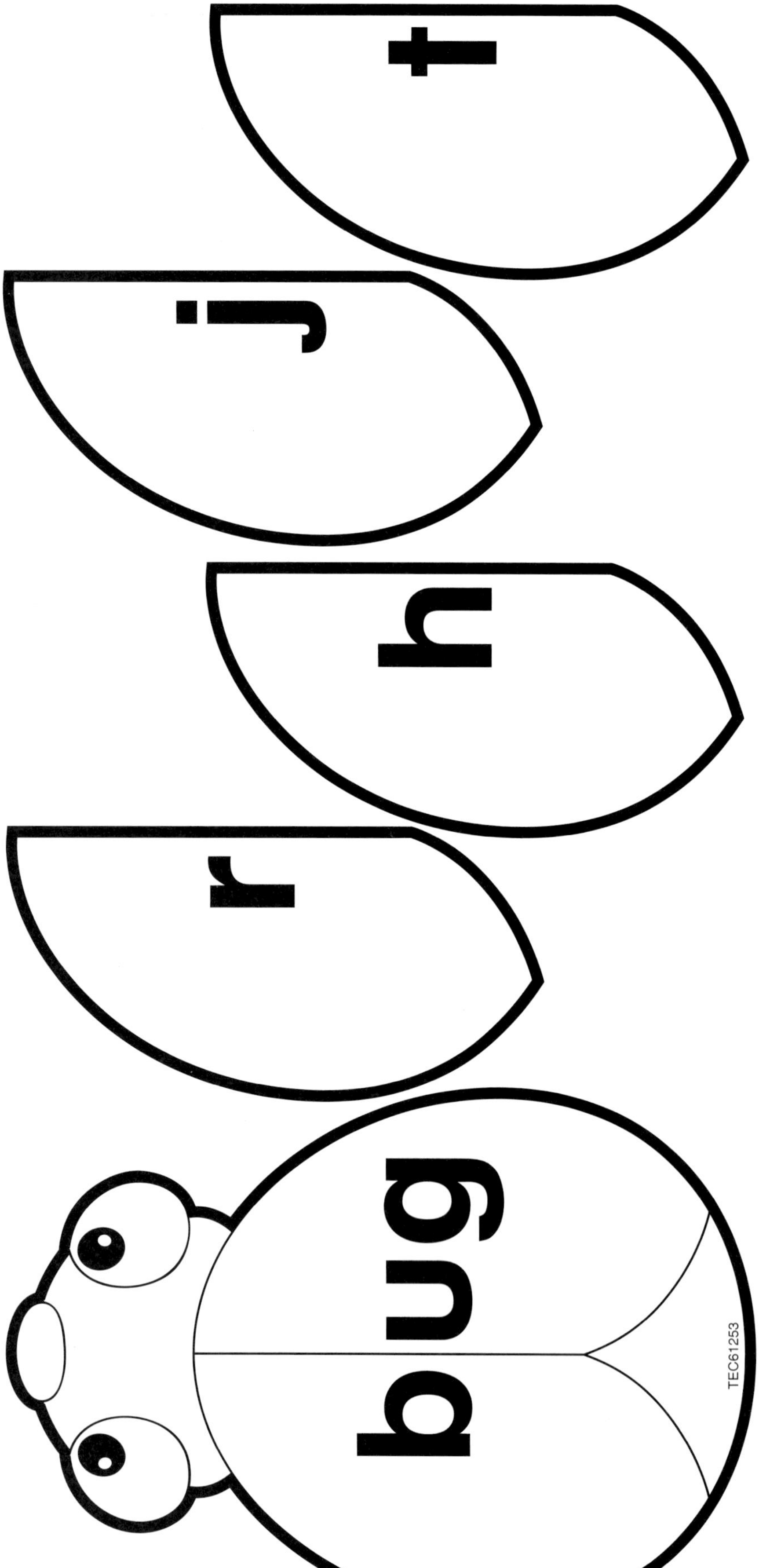

t

j

u

r

bug

TEC61253

Picture and Word Cards
Use with "An -ug Mug" on page 78.

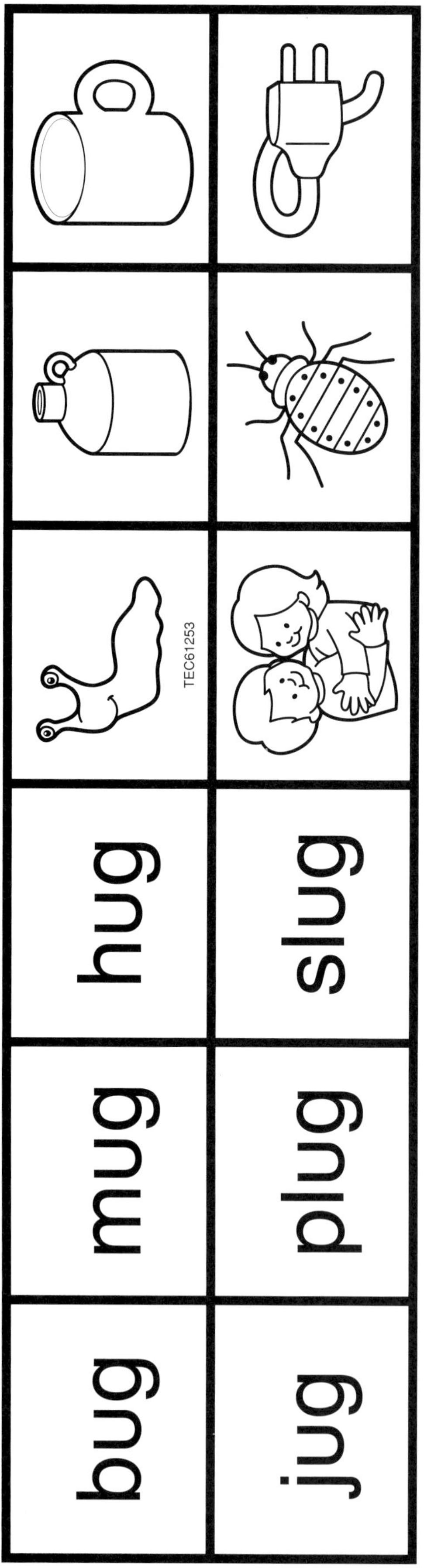

TEC61253

hug	slug
mug	plug
bug	jug

Word Family Helpers • ©The Mailbox® Books • TEC61253

Page 46
Order may vary.

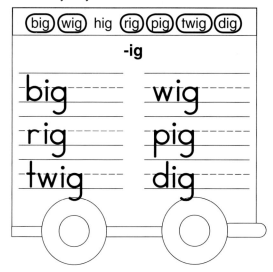

big (wig) hig (rig) pig (twig) dig

-ig

big   wig

rig   pig

twig   dig

Page 51

fin   grin

pin   twin

win   spin

Page 56

rip   hip

zip ship drip lip

Page 61

log dog
mog jog zog
hog rog fog frog

frog

hog   dog

log   jog   fog

Page 66

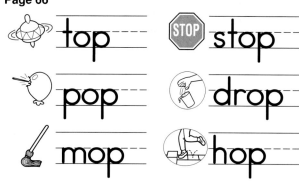

top   stop

pop   drop

mop   hop

Page 71

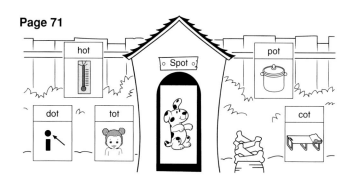

hot Spot pot
dot tot cot

Page 76
Order may vary.

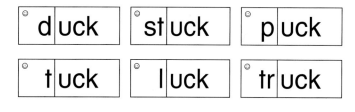

d|uck st|uck p|uck

t|uck l|uck tr|uck

Page 81

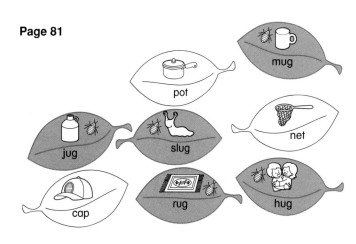

mug
pot
jug slug net
cap rug hug

Page 82

Page 83

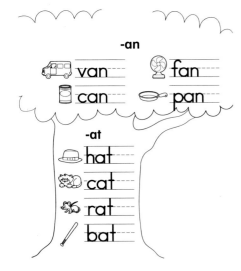

-an

van   fan
can   pan

-at

hat
cat
rat
bat

Page 84

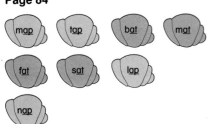

map   tap   bat   mat

fat   sat   lap

nap

Page 85

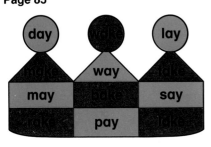

day   make   lay

make   way   take

may   bake   say

take   pay   lake

Page 86
Order may vary.

 -ed

red
fed
bed

 -et

wet
set
pet

Page 87

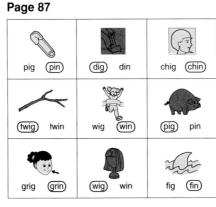

pig   (pin)   (dig)   din   chig   (chin)

(twig) twin   wig   (win)   (pig)   pin

grig   (grin)   (wig)   win   fig   (fin)

Page 88

dig   lip

pig   zip
twig   ship
wig   rip

Page 89
Order may vary.

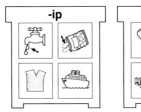 -ip   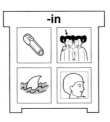 -in

Page 90
Order may vary.

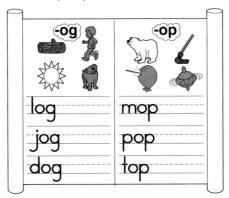

-og   -op

log   mop
jog   pop
dog   top

Page 91
Order may vary.

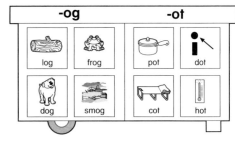

-og		-ot	
log	frog	pot	dot
dog	smog	cot	hot

Page 92

-op

hop
mop
drop

-ot

pot
dot
cot

Page 93

-uck   -ug

puck   rug
duck   mug
truck   bug